Marie Antoinette

A Captivating Guide to the Last Queen of France Before and During the French Revolution, Including Her Relationship with King Louis XVI

Free Bonus from Captivating History (Available for a Limited time)

Hi History Lovers!

Now you have a chance to join our exclusive history list so you can get your first history ebook for free as well as discounts and a potential to get more history books for free! Simply visit the link below to join.

Captivatinghistory.com/ebook

Also, make sure to follow us on:

Twitter: @Captivhistory

Facebook: Captivating History:@captivatinghistory

Contents

Introduction

Marie Antoinette is one of history's most celebrated queens thanks to her style and confidence, yet generally she is perceived as a greedy and selfish mistress of France. Born into a life of pure luxury as a Princess of Austria, Marie was very young when she was shipped abroad to await her turn as the Queen of France. She was forced all at once to come to terms with a foreign language, a different culture, and a court full of gossipy nobles who pounced at the first sign of weakness. Despite popular belief, Marie Antoinette was not entirely obsessed with pretty dresses and towering hairstyles—though she wouldn't quite have been the same without them.

Chapter 1 – An Archduchess is Born

By the time her daughter Maria Antonia Josepha Joanna of Austria-Lorraine was born on the second day of November 1755, motherhood was nothing special for the Empress Maria Theresa, ruler of the House of Habsburg. This was her fifteenth child and her eleventh daughter. One more child, Maximillian Franz, would be the last. Of the ten children who survived until adulthood, Maria Antonia—unexpectedly—would grow to become the most famous of the Austrian Empress and her husband, Francis I, ruler of the Holy Roman Empire.

Maria Antonia was born at her family home, the Imperial Apartments at the Hofburg Palace in Vienna, Austria. It is said that her busy mother went almost immediately back to the work of governance after her last daughter's birth, and the little girl was given into the care of a carefully-selected wet nurse. While proceedings in the royal house went along as usual, some members of the European public took the natural conditions of the baby's birth as ominous.

The first reason for unease surrounding the baby Maria Antonia was the actual date of her birth: November 2. During the 18th century, Catholic Europe followed the liturgical calendar that declared the second day of November All Souls Day. On this day, churches were swathed in black and mirrors were covered to prevent the souls of the dead in purgatory from re-entering the natural world. Church leaders required their subjects to pray for the souls of the dead so that those in purgatory might be forgiven their sins and find their way to Heaven.

All Souls Day was a time of superstition and fear of ghosts, and some of that fear and negativity was focused on the new royal baby. In addition to her somewhat foreboding birth date, the young Archduchess's godparents—Joseph I and Mariana Victoria, King and Queen of Portugal—were forced to leave their own crumbling palace in the midst of a terrible earthquake. If ever there were a sign from God that the newest Habsburg would suffer an ill fate, these events seemed to be just that.

Nevertheless, tiny Maria Antonia was born healthy and her Holy Roman Emperor father stopped to give his thanks, just as he did after the successful birth of every child. Furthermore, the youngest Archduchess of the family would outlive six of her own siblings.

Perhaps because she had up to four royal children in her care at one time, the child's governess, Countess von Brandeis, taught her charges no more than painting, singing and dancing. Whatever the reason typical lessons such as German, Italian and French were overlooked for several years, Maria Antonia quickly developed a reputation as a somewhat simpleminded girl. She loved to dance and play music, but as she began to frequent court as a child of 11 or 12, her knowledge of foreign languages was noted to be quite insufficient. She could not hold a proper conversation in any language but her own German, nor could she write in her own language.

Though these matters were of incredible importance for a royal family member who was likely to marry outside of one's own country, it is possible that as the penultimate child of 16, Maria Antonia's lessons were simply considered unnecessary. After all, there were only so many royal matches to be made, and Empress

Maria Theresa had her hopes pinned on the older Maria Elisabeth, born in 1743. Maria Elisabeth was considered the most attractive Habsburg daughter and therefore the most obvious choice for marital deals. Though the Empress had already borne four daughters, two of these had died in infancy and the third suffered a deformity that cost her all hope of marriage. The fourth, Maria Christina, born in 1742, is said to have been her mother's favorite daughter; As such, she was allowed to marry a man of her own choosing and forego the tedious rituals of a royal match.

By the time Maria Antonia was proposed as a potential bride for the Dauphin of France, her sister Maria Christina was in her mid-twenties and being considered as a potential bride for the widowed King of France. The latter had been withheld from many potential marriages during her youth because her family was always holding out for a better, more impressive, match. It was almost made with French king Louis XV, but before the wedding could go forward, the young woman contracted smallpox. She survived but was scarred badly enough to put a stop to all marriage plans once and for all.

As a young child, Maria Antonia's interests were mostly based in music. The German composer Christoph Willibald Gluck tutored her and helped the girl develop a beautiful singing voice as well as the ability to play the harp, the harpsichord, and the flute. The young Maria Antonia is reported to have regaled her family with songs in the evenings before she was engaged to the Dauphin of France at age fourteen. Music would be a lifelong passion that began early. When a young Wolfgang Amadeus Mozart visited the Austrian court to perform in 1762, he is said to have kissed the little Archduchess and proclaimed his wish to marry her.

When the engagement to the French Dauphin was made official, a royal tutor was sent from the French court to help educate the soon-to-be-Consort of France in the ways of the French royal court. At first attempt, tutor Abbé Vermond was hugely disappointed in the lack of Marie Antonia's education in literature, language, and history. As his lessons progressed, however, he saw that the girl was not a lost cause.

Said Abbé Vermond:

> She has a most graceful figure; holds herself well; and if (as may be hoped) she grows a little taller, she will have all the good qualities one could wish for in a great princess. Her character, her heart, are excellent.... She is much more intelligent than is generally supposed. Unfortunately, up to the age of twelve, she has not been trained to concentrate in any way. She is rather lazy and extremely frivolous; she is hard to teach. During the first six weeks, I inculcated her with the elements of literature, and found that she understood me very well when I gave her proper explanations. Then, she usually manifested a very sound judgment...

Chapter 2 – Maria Antonia Becomes Marie Antoinette

Vermond struggled to educate his Austrian pupil in the aftermath of the Seven Years' War. France and Austria had formalized their cooperation just one year after the birth of Maria Antonia, in the form of the Treaty of Versailles. This document sealed an agreement between the two countries to come to one another's aid in the event of an attack by Great Britain or Prussia. It was largely unprecedented since Austria and France were long-time enemies, particularly in land battles, but Empress Maria Theresa was unsatisfied with her country's existing alliance with Great Britain. She decided to seek new, potentially more powerful, alliances that would help her to recover lost Austrian lands.

Only two years after the treaty was signed, both Austria and France found themselves siding against both Great Britain and Prussia in an international war that engulfed Europe. At its roots, the Seven Years' War was a proxy conflict for all nations except Great Britain and France, ancient enemies who were once again squabbling over land rights in the American colonies. As an official ally of France, Austria was involved immediately and used the opportunity to reclaim Silesia, a piece of the modern Czech Republic that had been conquered by Prussia in 1742—ironically with the help of France. All of Europe had something at stake, and so the fighting continued with gusto until Britain achieved its major goals and the Treaty of Paris was signed in 1763. Silesia was not recovered.

During the time when teenaged Maria Antonia was receiving her French education in Austria, her country was no longer battling alongside France and therefore the written alliance of the two countries felt strained. A marriage was particularly important to solidify the friendship between nations who had fought against each other so often in the previous three centuries. Mathieu-Jacques de Vermond had a bigger job than it seemed on the surface; if he could not train his Austrian Archduchess how to communicate properly with her French court, her strong accent and foreign manners would make her an easy target for the French public. In short, if the tutor failed to produce a passable French Consort to the crown, the very purpose of the marriage could be undermined.

The Duchesse de Gramont, sister of France's envoy to Austria in charge of dowry negotiations, was given the job of physically transforming Maria Antonia. The Archduchess was of the highest nobility in name and breeding, but her manner of dress and social interaction was not exemplary. As difficult as it may be to believe that one of the world's most renown fashion icons was anything but perfectly-groomed, contemporary sources claimed that the princess wore wrinkled clothes and had unruly hair.

The first thing the Duchesse de Gramont did was change the young lady's undergarments. French ladies wouldn't dare be seen in public—or in private, for that matter—wearing anything under their elaborate dresses but the ubiquitous whalebone stay. These harsh, stiff corsets were designed to pinch in a woman's natural waist as much as possible, while creating a flawless straight line from waist to head. The girls understandably fought this transformation, but ultimately lost the battle.

Next, Maria Antonia's exceptionally crooked teeth needed fixing, and the answer was an early form of today's dental braces: Fauchard's Bandeau. The painful and awkward mechanism was endured for several months while the young Archduchess's teeth were squeezed into a more attraction assemblage. While she waited for the end of the process finally to come, the Austrian princess watched her wardrobe transform under the careful selective processes of the Duchesse de Gramont.

The French court considered itself the absolute height of modern fashion, and it was a genuine part of any incoming princess's role to continue to solidify that reputation. Once the Austrian girl was married and styled in the French way as Marie Antoinette, it wouldn't do just to wear satisfactory dresses and shoes—she would be expected to become an icon of nobility and fashion. There would even be an allotted part of her income dedicated to cultivating French style.

Maria Theresa was determined that her daughter would be at the top of the French king's list when it concerned marrying off his eldest grandson and heir, Louis XVI. To that end, the Empress made sure that everything possible was done to make Maria Antonia the equal of any French monarch. **She is said to have spent 400,000 livres on her daughter's trousseau**—at a time when the entire wardrobe of the average noble cost about 2,000 livres.

Another French stylist was invited to Vienna to work on the princess's transformation: Larsenneur. A famous hairdresser, Larsenneur had been responsible for the trend-setting hairstyle of Louis XV's mistress, Madame du Pompadour. The hair expert was not simply there to turn a normal head of hair into a spectacle; he was summoned to help correct bald patches along the girl's hairline and find a way to deal with her unkempt reddish-blond curls. The solution was a low-lying upsweep to disguise the bare skin and keep her forehead from appearing too large. It was powdered and decorated with jewels.

The girl's countless elaborate gowns were all French style, low-necked to expose the top of a woman's breasts. Bodices were constructed low and to a point along the wearer's torso, culminating in huge floor-length skirts and many layers of petticoats underneath. Sleeves were long, puffed, and adorned with ribbons or gems. The dresses were heavy and by no means designed for comfort or outdoor pursuits.

When Marie Antoinette emerged from the labors of so many French stylists and physicians, she was perfect for her role as a member of the French monarchy. Amazingly, she would take the fashions of her new country even further once she became its queen.

Chapter 3 - The Dauphine

Corseted, dressed, coiffed, and sporting lovely straight teeth, Maria Antonia was finally considered a proper and fitting bride for the French heir to the throne. She could grapple her way through the French language enough to manage soft-spoken, usually silent, politeness to her in-laws and members of the aristocracy; it was time, finally, to get married.

As lovely as she appeared on her wedding day on April 19, 1770, Maria Antonia was never even glimpsed by her groom. Neither, of course, did she see Louis-Auguste. As was perfectly normal at the time, the two royals were wed in a proxy ceremony in Vienna.

The bride wore a beautiful silver gown with a long train and entered the Church of the Augustine Friars at 6:00 p.m. It was the same place her parents had been married, 34 years earlier. In place of her bridegroom, Maria Antonia had as proxy her own brother, the Archduke Ferdinand. The two went through their vows together with the Papal Nuncio, Monsignor Visconti, and afterward went to the formal wedding dinner. Ferdinand was required to sit at his sister's side for the entire evening.

Celebrations continued for days, and the new fourteen-year-old bride began her journey to France two days after the ceremony. She met her fifteen-year-old husband in the French forest of Compiegne for a stiff and formal introduction. Just as the journey was portrayed in the 2006 movie "Marie Antoinette," the Austrian princess did indeed stop on the Austrian-French border to change clothes. Though she had already conformed to the most haute-couture French fashions, the girl's new royal in-laws demanded that she only wear dress, shoes, undergarments, and accessories that were made in France itself. Therefore, in a makeshift tent in the midst of Compiegne, Maria Antonia was stripped of all the physical adornments she had known as a member of the Austrian royalty and dressed again in French clothing selected by the entourage that accompanied Louis XV and his grandson.

When Louis XVI's bride emerged and crossed into France, she became Marie Antoinette.

There was a French ceremony at the Palace of Versailles on the 16th of May, 1770, with lavish food, drink, and guests. Dressed in their finest garments, Louis XVI and Marie Antoinette walked together to the Royal Chapel, followed by King Louis XV and his sons. This time, it was the groom who wore a suit of silver; the bride was dressed in a gown of lilac. The official ceremony was performed by Archbishop Reims, followed by the signing of the registry. Afterward, the newlyweds proceeded to Versailles's famous Hall of Mirrors, which was beautiful and brightly-lit for the occasion.

There were many functions to attend once the official wedding had been concluded, including multiple receptions. The largest boasted as many as 5,000 attendees and took place in the brand-new Royal Opera House.

After the first day of festivities, both young people were ceremoniously put to bed together, as was routine, to be sure of marital consummation. History tells us that the king ceremoniously presented his grandson with the latter's nightshirt; the Duchess of Chartres presented the bride with hers. The couple climbed into the bed together to prove their intention and then the bed curtains were closed. Exhausted, the young couple did nothing but fall asleep.

The royal marriage was celebrated for another two weeks in Paris and Versailles, until on the 30th of May, **an accident with a**

fireworks display led to the deaths of 132 people. The tragedy at the Place de la Concorde was considered a terrible omen for the marriage, and the bride and groom were so upset about it that they used their combined monthly allowance to provide help for the families of victims.

Being an Austrian Dauphine was always going to be a difficult job, given the shared past of France and Austria. But on the other hand, the French always admired a beautiful, well-turned-out noble, so when Marie Antoinette made her public debut that June, she was generally accepted and praised by the commoners. Her presence at Versailles, however, was possibly more intimidating than any public appearance.

One of the first problems the young princess encountered was the issue of King Louis XV's mistress, Madame du Barry. After marriage negotiations between Marie Antoinette's sister and the king fell through, no more were taken seriously; this meant that effectively, du Barry was treated like the French Queen by her lover and his close companions. In fact, the king's mistress was called the *maîtresse-en-titre*—essentially, the favorite mistress of the king. As such, she was entitled to her own apartments and the respect of fellow courtiers.

Since Madame du Barry (by birth Marie-Jeanne Bécu) was not of noble birth, and because she had been a high-class courtesan (a prostitute), the beloved mistress of the king was scorned by most of the noblewomen at Versailles. When Marie Antoinette moved into her own apartments at the palace, she was approached by her new husband's aunts on the subject. They told her by no means to speak with du Barry, and she agreed that was the best way forward.

Unfortunately, the teenaged princess was not only receiving advice from her French family but her Austrian one as well. Her mother wrote her letters describing the personal benefits of a friendship with Madame du Barry, stating that such a comradery would make her a favorite of the king's. The Austrian ambassador to France, Comte de

Mercy-Argenteau, agreed heartily with the girl's mother, with whom he frequently exchanged letters. Meanwhile, du Barry herself had begun to complain to the king that the Dauphine was snubbing her; the two of them became the topic of hot gossip throughout the palace.

In a passionate bid for her daughter to appease the ego of the king's mistress, Maria Theresa convinced Marie Antoinette to finally speak to du Barry on New Year's Day, 1772. Her words were far from notable, and yet they were indeed noted: "**There are a lot of people at Versailles today.**" The passing comment apparently appeased Madame du Barry, and the two continued on happily, for the most part, in separate social circles.

Chapter 4 – Queen at Nineteen

In just a few short years as France's Dauphine, Marie Antoinette was thrust further into the political spotlight when reigning King Louis XV died. It was 10 May 1774 when Marie Antoinette and Louis-Auguste became the Queen and King of France and Navarre.

By 1774, King Louis XV had ruled France for 59 years, and though he was not a young man, he had not been in poor health prior to that year. In the month before his death, the king quickly fell ill and was discovered to have contracted smallpox. At first, physicians believed the king could pull through; they lanced his pox and administered blood-lettings to remove the disease from his body. The royal family were strictly instructed not to go near the sick man's apartments to avoid contagion. The elder Louis seemed stable for a time, but by the May 8th it became apparent to Louis XV's swarm of top doctors that he was not going to beat the sickness. He died on the afternoon of the 10th.

As is tradition, the king's retinue raced to the apartments of the dead king's son to announce the death of his father. Also, to proclaim, "Long live the King!" According to Madame Campan, one of Marie Antoinette's ladies in waiting, the young couple was very emotional at the news. At the sound of the courtiers rushing from the old king's apartments, Marie and Louis knew at once what had happened and both fell to their knees. She reportedly said, **"God! Guide us; protect us. We are too young to reign."**

Nevertheless, the parade of court life carried on without a moment's pause. The new king and queen were asked to enter their own grand salon so that dignitaries might pay their respects. They did so, Marie Antoinette holding a handkerchief to her eyes as she leaned on Louis-Auguste.

In the days following the old king's death, Louis-Auguste began to assemble trusted advisors to help him rule the country. He made several appointments to the various ministries of his government and brought in a new Prime Minister: Jean-Frédéric Phélypeaux, Comte de Maurepas. As for Madame du Barry, she was exiled from Versailles, never to return.

At first, the Queen of France and Navarre left the governing to her husband and his advisors. Louis-August gave his wife an estate all her own: the Petit Trianon. This was a small chateau, built by Louis XV on the grounds of Versailles especially for his deceased mistress, Madame du Pompadour. After her death, the estate was occupied by Madame du Barry. The young queen adored her new property and frequented it as often as possible. She spent her time chiefly at Petit Trianon, craving the privacy of the little home, while Louis XVI struggled to learn statesmanship.

The king had inherited an immense national debt from his father, yet he had also been taught to spend liberally. Above all, he desired the love of his people, and these three aspects of Louis's kingship were difficult to consolidate. He trusted that his own household budgets were set properly and followed them as well as he could manage, focusing his energy mostly on the notion of religious freedom.

At that time, France was in religious turmoil as Roman Catholicism was the only officially legal religion in the country. Nevertheless, France was inhabited by a minority of Huguenots, Jews, and Lutherans who could not marry unless they converted to Catholicism. Louis XVI desired tolerance for all religious beliefs, which was a timely wish given that France was home to many great philosophers who not only practiced non-Catholic religions but often believed in atheism. To subdue the conflict, the king signed the Edict of Versailles, allowing all French people to practice their own religion and marry without being Catholic. This document was nicknamed the **Edict of Tolerance**, something that must have made the young king particularly proud.

Marie Antoinette was unconcerned with the politics of the day, though she took her role as a fashion icon very seriously. She lavishly ordered dresses, shoes, and accompaniments for herself and all her ladies in waiting, most famously choosing to clothe herself and her ladies in English-style gowns made from previously-illegal fabric. This offending fabric, Indienne, was a reproduction of original printed fabrics and textiles that came from India. King Louis XV believed he had a vested interest in the Indienne fabrics ban of 1686 and had attacked the issue vehemently. The illegality of such fabric was based on the idea that their import (though much of the reproduction work was in fact done in Marseilles) endangered France's existing silk and wool industries. Fully aware that French manufacturers were creating knock-offs, he outlawed those as well, demanding that only single-color fabrics were suitable.

The **Fabric Wars** did nothing to change the French nobility's taste for printed fabric, and the law was fairly unsuccessful in changing their purchase behavior. By 1759, the king repealed the law, spurring a wave of updated French fashions full of printed fabrics that Marie Antoinette and her entourage took for granted. Her favorite designers and vendors frequented Versailles and the Petit Trianon with armloads of silk, wool, furs, and printed cotton with which to create the most elaborate gowns, shoes, hair ribbons, and necklaces.

While the queen busied herself with textile selection, interior design, and garden sculpting, the common French laborer remained poor and without much hope for the future. Almost immediately from the start of her tenure as queen, Marie Antoinette set herself apart from the common people in an extreme and—to some—garish manner. One could not help but notice the extravagance and expensive qualities of her dress and environment, and she became a sore subject of gossip throughout France.

Nevertheless, the young Queen of France had been taught little else but to ensure that she was beautiful and exuded an air of utmost sophistication. So, she continued to fill her wardrobes and jewelry cases and present herself as just the person her mother and French stylists had insisted she become when she was fourteen years old and about to marry the Dauphin. She even called her old music teacher, Christoph Willibald Gluck, into her service.

For Marie Antoinette, becoming the Queen of all France was understandably shocking and frightening, but the teenaged girl truly came into her own once the assets of the country were put at her fingertips. For the first few years of hers and Louis XVI's reign, it was only the latter who took on the true burdens of monarchy.

Chapter 5 – A Marriage at Odds with Itself

France's young monarchs had benefits that other royal couples did not—for one, they were of a similar age and both were virgins when they married. Additionally, since the couple was married quite early, they didn't experience any particular pressure to start a family right away. They were simply a young married couple living at Versailles, ideally preparing for their future roles as King and Queen of France.

Unfortunately, apart from their nobility, Marie and Louis had little in common and were not immediately drawn to one another. Louis was considered shy, while his wife was naturally vivacious and social. Once she had come to terms with her new surroundings and felt confident with the French language, Marie Antoinette blossomed at Versailles. She made friends, had parties, played cards, gambled, gossiped, and was a very popular figure at the palace.

The king, on the other hand, was quieter and much more introverted than Marie. He had a passion for locksmith work and enjoyed hunting. Louie is even said to have befriended the royal carpenter and learned how to make furniture. He went to bed hours earlier than Marie, who stayed up until the small hours of the morning at her parties. As it was customary for married nobles to occupy different bedrooms—and in Louis and Marie's case, different houses—the couple did not spend much time together. Louis went off on hunting expeditions and met with government appointees and foreign dignitaries; Marie talked with her friends, played games, and spent her time at Petit Trianon. Louis sat by the fireside reading books from his library of 8,000 volumes; Marie gave him excuses so that she could stay up late with her friends.

There was little chance of the two growing close as friends or married partners, apart from their formal appearances together at the breakfast table and state dinners. Nevertheless, the couple was not considered cold, simply awkward. Louis gave his wife countless presents, including a **hand-crafted spinning wheel** he made himself. She was not a good candidate for such a gift, however, since she left the spinning and sewing to her attendants and contracted designers. She gave the gift to one of her attendants.

One of the most troubling issues that divided the queen and the king was that of government. As Marie grew older, she and her own advisors showed interest in the affairs of France, to the point where the queen attempted to appoint her own people as the king's counselors.

The *Gentleman's Magazine,* 1776:

> The Queen commenced the action by proposing it to the King; but he told her in plain terms; that he had good and able counsellors; that he meant to act in all things for the benefit of his people, (*and this alone is his real object*); and desired she would mine her own department, and not interfere in matters of states.

Adamant that he alone would see to the business of ruling France, King Louis XVI even had his wife's counselors removed from Versailles. She became very upset and ill; when the king visited her, they rehashed the same argument and neither was satisfied. This was one of the most troubling ways the personalities of the royal couple clashed, since the after-effects were so far-reaching. An intelligent young woman may have been an asset to King Louis XVI, especially since in retrospect the latter cannot be accused of having ruled

France as effectively as needed. Nevertheless, Marie Antoinette was not allowed to dabble in politics of the day, and so she focused her efforts on the matters to which Louis appointed her: helping mothers, children, and the less fortunate throughout the country.

Despite not becoming a mother for some time, it was obvious Marie Antoinette loved children, and she actually adopted some of the orphans left by deceased employees at Versailles. Her husband was kind-hearted and charitable as well, and the pair of them established several charity organizations during their reign. The desire to give was perhaps the strongest bond Louis and Marie shared. Though no one would ever accuse Marie and Louis of being passionate lovers, the two did share a special bond in their acts of charity.

Before she became queen, Marie Antoinette ironically made a name for herself in France as a woman disinterested in unnecessary expense. This was thanks to her request to King Louis XV that the French public not be bothered with the customary **Queen's Belt tax**, a tax that came into effect every time a new queen ascended the throne. She had heard talk of this particular tax being too much for some poorer people to handle and therefore convinced her king not to ask it of anyone. The public was very grateful and impressed, as was Marie's young husband.

Together, Marie and Louis were one of the most benevolent royal couples in history, though they would not be remembered that way. Louis founded the *Maison Philanthropique,* of which he and his wife were patrons. The organization aided the elderly, blind, and widowed. Marie, for her part, established a home for unwed mothers on the very grounds of Versailles. Every evening, free food was laid in the palace itself for all who desired it. In addition, Marie was responsible for a project in which several cottages were built within the grounds of Versailles to house to house poor families.

In serving and protecting several poor families and orphaned children within their estate, the king and queen demonstrated their true inclination to peace, fraternity, and the wellbeing of the nation.

In this respect, Marie and Louis were a united, healthy couple who worked well together. Still, the country remained in debt and the aristocracy waited eight years for the Royals to produce an heir to the throne of France.

Chapter 6 – The Issue of Heirs

Few things about Marie Antoinette have captured the public's imagination quite like her bedroom habits with Louis-Auguste. Since the couple was married relatively early in life, the Queen of France was politely allowed a few years to mature before she was expected to bring a new member of the royal family into the world. Once the old king died, however, the pressure was on to give birth—and to do it soon.

In fact, Marie Antoinette would not produce a child until 1778, when she was twenty-three years old. By that time, the country was rife with gossip concerning the love life of the king and queen, not to mention the specific problems they must be having behind closed bed curtains. We can never know exactly what happened between the royal couple, or what medical issues may have delayed Marie's pregnancy, but there is still plenty of speculation on the subject.

The most prominent theory is that King Louis XVI had the fault, either physically or mentally. Some speculated that the shy, withdrawn Louis was simply too anxious to consummate the marriage. Still more reasoned that there must be a physical problem with the king, such as phimosis—a condition in which the foreskin of a man's penis cannot be pulled down from the glans. Though sexual intercourse is possible with this condition, it can be very painful which could explain why a sufferer would choose not to engage in sex.

Louis-Auguste had been closely examined by his father's personal doctor in 1770 to check for any obvious physical reason that the Dauphin could not produce an heir. **The doctor** noted that everything was as it should be, a report that has made many historians believe that the young Dauphin did not have phimosis.

Two years after this report, the king summoned Marie and his grandson and demanded a frank conversation about their marital relationship. The Dauphin explained to the king that he had attempted to consummate his marriage but that intense pain stopped him. Concerned, the king brought his personal physician, Joseph de Lassone, to examine the French prince. On record, the doctor reported, like his predecessor, that the Dauphine had no impediment to marital consummation.

Rumor, however, did not agree with the official statement from Lassone. Instead, gossip held that the heir to the French throne did indeed have a physical deformity that required surgical correction.

The Spanish Ambassador to France, Count Aranda, mentioned the issue in extraordinary detail in one of his letters, dated **5 August 1774**:

> Some say the frenum is so short that the prepuce does not retract upon entry, causing His Majesty much pain and forcing him to curtail the movements necessary to complete the act. Others think a tight prepuce prevents the head of the penis from being exposed, making it impossible for His Majesty to have full erections. If it's a matter of a short frenum, this condition is found in many individuals, causing problems when they first become sexually active; but since most people have a stronger sex drive than His Majesty (a reflection of his temperament or inexperience), they manage—with practice, a groan

of pain and some good will—to tear the frenum completely, or sufficiently to keep using it, so that gradually intercourse becomes normal. But when the patient is timid, the surgeon makes a small incision, doing away with the obstacle. If the problem is a tight prepuce, one could resort to an operation which at the king's age is more painful and severe, requiring a kind of circumcision, because if the rough edges of the lips of the incision are not made smooth, intercourse could be impossible.

There is still yet another theory on the marital affairs of Louis and Marie, this one quite new. Scholar **Simone Bertiere**, after reading archived letters sent between Empress Maria Theresa and the Hapsburg Ambassador at Versailles, came to the conclusion that both Marie Antoinette and Louis-Auguste suffered physical attributes that made their sexual encounters extremely painful. She describes these conditions as "bracquemart assez considérable" and "l'étroitesse du chemin" respectively, an oversized penis and an uncommonly narrow vagina.

In 1777, Marie Antoinette's brother paid her and Louis a visit. Since their father's death in 1765, Joseph II had been the Holy Roman Emperor and one of the most important rulers in Europe. He took it upon himself to talk with his royal brother-in-law and figure out why there were still no French heirs. After their first discussion on the subject, Joseph II declared that the pair were "blunderers" who lacked technique. **Of Louis, he said**: "He has strong erections, he inserts his member, remains there for perhaps two minutes without moving, withdraws without ejaculating, and while still erect, bids good night."

Louis expressed his wish to perform his marital duty but told Joseph II that other than making children, he had no real urge to have sex at all. The latter gave Louis the basic education he believed was necessary and hoped for the best. Two months later, **Marie wrote to her mother** and proclaimed the deed had finally been done. On his part, Louis admitted: "I delight in the pleasure, and I regret that I wasn't aware of it for so long."

Finally, the couple could get down to the business of producing heirs to the Bourbon line. Before a year passed, Marie Antoinette was pregnant with daughter Marie Therese. The child was born in 1778. Louis Joseph arrived in 1781, then Louis Charles in 1785, and finally Sophie Helene Beatrix in 1786.

Not all of Louis-August and Marie Antoinette's children would survive to the French Revolution.

Chapter 7 - Madame Deficit

Marie Antoinette's lavish spending habits as queen were so well-known and so loathed by a country in extreme debt and poverty that she became known as Madame Deficit. She was caricatured constantly as a selfish, spoiled woman who couldn't stop spending money on her hair, her wardrobe, her shoes, her gardens, and on spectacular foods. As the years of Marie and Louis' reign progressed, the people forgot that their queen had foregone the Queen's Belt tax. They didn't congratulate their monarchs for hosting evening meals at Versailles or building cottages for peasants on those very grounds. All they knew was that the price of bread was ridiculous and the queen was swimming in luxury—not to mention bread.

In truth, the royal family of France was mindful of the state of poverty among most of its people. They attempted to make cutbacks to their personal budgets as often as possible, instead funneling that money into a variety of charitable organizations. While many needy people were indeed benefitting from these funds, the bulk of France saw no difference whatsoever to its situation. They blamed both monarchs but Marie Antoinette in particular.

She was an easy target, first because of her expensive tastes and second because she was Austrian. Her husband was also an easy target because of the widespread belief that he was impotent. The royal couple were often depicted in satirical journals as a flaccid penis and a trussed-up floozy holding its reins.

It is true, of course, that the last French queen spent money lavishly. Seemingly without a second thought, she undertook landscaping and renovation projects throughout Versailles. In particular, she focused on the refurbishment of her special property, the Petit Trianon. At the little chateau, Marie Antoinette often hosted her close friends and showered them with food, drink, dresses, and other presents. Her lifestyle was by no means affordable or even within the imagination of most French citizens.

Despite her efforts to meet her own budgets, Marie Antoinette failed to keep track of her spending, only becoming aware of an over-expenditure by a word from her husband or advisors. Her clothing budget, in estimated current buying power, equated to about US $3.6 million—and yet, some years she spent up to double that. When prodded, the queen would request that another part of her allowance be used to make up the difference, or she would have the king pay for it out of his own personal spending money.

Perhaps she believed that the excessive amount of money she spent on her wardrobe and other personal projects was anything but, as of course those funds were going straight into the hands of artisans, architects, laborers, and the like. Still, as much money as Marie Antoinette allocated towards her designers and builders, little was being done to alleviate the poverty in which most French people spent their lives. Something more proactive needed to be done, most likely in the shape of tax reform. Unfortunately, Louis was adamantly in charge of governance and none of the reforms he made seemed to quite make enough difference.

Through his reign, Louis-Auguste faced opposition to his ideas from the Parliament of Paris. They refused to allow a tax on landowners and the nobility, who considered themselves above such things through an ancient blood right. The nobility, via the Parliament, insisted that their service to France was in war and other **"noble** acts." Nevertheless, the king **reduced his household multiple times**, awarded French rights to non-Catholics living in France, and lowered general taxes over several years. He simultaneously abolished servitude—akin to serfdom and slavery—first on royal lands and then in the whole of France. Still, these efforts did not take public pressure off the French monarchs.

One of the most hated of the Queen's projects was *La Hameau de la Reine*±The Hamlet of the Queen. This was an extension of the land around the Petit Trianon, on which Marie designed and contracted the construction of a little rural village around a man-made lake. Her first step was to install the **English Gardens** as a replacement for the old king's botanical gardens, which she felt were outdated. Architect Richard Mique built two structures for the gardens: The Love Monument and the Belvedere.

A few years after the gardens were completed, the queen had the new lake dug out and filled. It was to be surrounded by a model village that fit a contemporary aristocratic trend to build overwrought, undersized structures called "follies." Follies were particularly in vogue in England, which explains the French Queen's addition of the English Gardens alongside her miniature village.

The Hamlet featured several small cottages with rustic exteriors and richly-decorated interiors where the queen could host small groups of friends. There were also vegetable gardens, a folly windmill (just for decoration,) a dairy, and a little farm filled with well-groomed sheep, pigs, horses, and hens. The queen liked to dress in simple country-style gowns and spend time in her hamlet gathering eggs, milking goats, and teaching her children about the animals and plants within the estate.

Perhaps her habit of pretending to be a peasant was the worst thing for Marie Antoinette at the time, given the state of the rest of France. While she and her children and friends dressed in inexpensive clothing and laughed their way through a make-believe rustic village, people in real villages relied on their actual farms, mills, and livestock to fill their hungry stomachs. Worst of all, the village at Versailles cost untold *livres* that could have been spent in any number of productive ways for the country.

Disgusted at the entire project, the French public decided there must be some better reason for the Queen's elaborate village than mere education and parties. The especially wondered about the purpose of a secret passage to the garden's grotto and speculated heavily.

A popular theory was that Madame Deficit, tired of her husband's inability to perform in the bedroom, used the *Hameau de la Reine* and gardens to meet with secrets lovers—one in particular.

Chapter 8 – Count Axel von Ferson

If there was one man the French public could have bet on visiting the queen at her English Gardens, it was Count Hans Axel von Ferson. Born the same year as Marie Antoinette, von Ferson was a member of the Swedish nobility. The two met in 1774 at the Royal Opera House during a masked ball. They would not see each other again until 1778, at Versailles.

Von Ferson was a Marshall of the Realm of Sweden and a General of Horse in the Royal Swedish Army. He served in Sweden until 1778 when he traveled back to France to check in on an army training camp. Marie Antoinette, whose status had changed from Dauphine to Queen of France, remembered him clearly from their earlier meeting. She made an effort to include the count in her social engagements, as is evident from the **journal of Count Axel von Ferson**:

> *August 26: Last Tuesday I went to Versailles to be presented to the royal family. The queen, who is charming, said when she saw me, 'Ah! Here is an old acquaintance.' The rest of the family did not say a word to me.*

> *September 8: The queen, who is the prettiest and most amiable princess that I know, has had the kindness to*

inquire about me often; she asked Creutz why I did not go to her card parties on Sundays; and hearing that I did go one Sunday when there was none, she sent me a sort of excuse. Her pregnancy advances and is quite visible.

November 19: The queen treats me with great kindness; I often pay her my court at her card-games, and each time she makes to me little speeches that are full of good-will. As someone had told her of my Swedish uniform, she expressed a wish to see me in it; I am to go Thursday thus dressed, not to Court, but to the queen's apartments. She is the most amiable princess that I know.

That same year, France's military was getting ready to head to America and battle its historic enemy—Great Britain—by proxy in the Revolutionary War. Von Ferson was prepared to fight on the part of France, and he did so two years later in 1780. His official position was aide-de-camp to General Rochambeau, who took him to the east coast of America. The General and his aide-de-camp eventually met with George Washington in September of 1780 at Hartford, Connecticut, before marching south to join with other regiments.

The great military man's career kept him busy and often away from France altogether, but in 1784 he returned to Versailles for a short time with Gustavus III from Germany. During the visit, the count sat at Marie Antoinette's side and promised that when he returned from his upcoming trip to Sweden he would have a dog for her. He did just that and the queen named her new pet Odin.

As Count Axel von Fersen traveled, he and the French Queen kept up contact regularly through letters. Clearly, theirs was a strong friendship—but officially, there never seemed any legitimate proof of an extramarital affair on the part of Marie Antoinette. Letters were made public, but these revealed nothing untoward.

Rumors persist to this day, however, that the queen and her favorite count were indeed having an affair—one that may have produced the queen's last child, Sophie. The most compelling argument for this theory comes from Evelyn Farr, a biographer who tracked down unseen letters between not only Marie and Hans but also their go-betweens.

According to Farr's research, the secretive couple used many techniques to hide the fact that they were romantically entangled: codes, codenames, invisible ink, secret seals, and double envelopes. Thanks to the renewed search efforts on the part of Farr, as well as less-than-trustworthy couriers used by Marie and von Ferson, a seemingly subverted truth has been revealed.

The queen ends a letter to her friend with particular emotion, dated **4 January 1792**: "I am going to close, but not without telling you, my dear and very tender friend, that I love you madly and never, ever could I exist a moment without adoring you."

For his part, the count was equally full of emotion in a letter dated 25 October 1791: "My dear and very tender friend – my God, how cruel it is to be so close and not be able to see each other! … I live and exist only to love you; adoring you is my only consolation."

Evelyn Farr knows that other historians prefer not to draw conclusions from expressions like these—the French are known for their romantic language, after all. Resistance to her hypothesis aside, Farr said is convinced. She uncovered one letter in which von Fersen said "I love you madly." As Farr notes,

> 'I love you madly' is a very strong phrase—you don't say that to a good friend. It's really telling; it implies a physical relationship. They were lovers. From what the Duke of Dorchester insinuated to the Duchess of Devonshire, it was fairly obvious Sophie was Fersen's child.

Whatever the true relationship between Marie Antoinette and Count Axel von Fersen, the former used the full extent of his influence to try to sneak the royal family out of France and into Austria at the onset of the Revolution. After Marie Antoinette's death, the count was unmistakably affected. He wrote to his sister on the subject in **1793**: "I have lost everything I had in this world. . . . The one I loved so much, for whom I would have given my life a thousand times over, is no more."

The count continued his military career after the French queen's death, returning to Sweden where he supported the claim of Gustavus IV's son as heir to the throne. His faction was not much favored next to the Crown Prince Charles August, and when the prince died in von Fersen's presence, rumors broke out that it was an inside job. Count Hans Axel von Fersen was killed by an angry mob on the day of Charles August's funeral, June 20, 1810.

Chapter 9 – The Lost Children

Marie Antoinette gave birth a total of four times between 1778 and 1786, to Marie Therese, Louis Joseph, Louis Charles, and Sophie Helene Beatrix.

After the birth of Marie's last child, the royals commissioned a family portrait by the popular painter **Élisabeth Vigée-Lebrun**. The painting, still hanging in the Palace of Versailles today, depicts Marie Antoinette in a lush red gown, seated with her feet on an embroidered cushion and baby Louis Charles on her lap. Marie Therese stands at her mother's right, leaning in and embracing the queen with a look of adoration. Louis Joseph stands on the opposite side of the portrait, a baby carriage between him and his mother. Louis Joseph gestures to the inside of the carriage—but it's empty.

Baby Sophie was meant to fill that carriage, making the portrait a complete representation of Marie Antoinette's motherhood. The painting was supposed to celebrate the royal family and present the queen to her people as an accomplished and caring mother— something they believed she was not. Unfortunately, while the painting was still in the works, the youngest member of the royal family contracted tuberculosis and passed away before her first birthday. It's unclear whether Vigée-Lebrun had to paint over the baby or if she simply left the unfinished carriage empty while finished the painting—but in either case it is a clear reminder of Marie and Louis' first lost child.

Louis Joseph was the eldest son; therefore, he was the heir apparent and the Dauphin of France. As the heir to the crown, Louis Joseph had his own household and a multitude of staff from the moment he was born. His education was of the utmost importance and happily the young boy was considered very bright for his age.

At the age of three, the Dauphin became seriously ill and to keep him safe from infections and public sickness, he was sent to his father's private property at Chateau de la Muette. The boy did in fact recover and return to Versailles. Soon afterward, he returned to the Chateau de la Muette to be inoculated against smallpox.

Though Edward Jenner's smallpox vaccine had only been about for ten years, the French royals had lost enough family members to the disease to risk an early form of inoculation. Louis Joseph received particles from smallpox sores either into his open skin or through his nasal cavity. In this manner, the Dauphin was ideally exposed to enough of the disease to form a small-scale infection, thus immunizing him from a case of full-fledged smallpox after his recovery. The treatment was successful.

The next year, Louis Joseph received new tutors—men, to replace the governess—and his education took a more serious role in his daily routine. Unfortunately, the five-year-old Dauphin began to suffer from high fevers that became progressively worse over the next two years. Marie Antoinette's eldest son died at the age of seven from severe tuberculosis. The year was 1789.

If Marie Antoinette was indeed having a romantic and sexual affair with her friend, Count Hans Axel von Fersen, Farr and other researchers suspect that the Swede may have been father to both Louis Charles and Princess Sophie. Nothing in the letters between the queen and Fersen mention the subject, though **a friend's letter to the British Prime Minister does**:

> I know him [Fersen] intimately and think him a man
> of unquestionable honor and veracity. He is calm,
> resolute, and uncommonly discreet, without being

reserved. This gentleman was Colonel of the Royal Suédois; was Her Most Christian Majesty's prime favorite; and is generally supposed to be the father of the present Dauphin.

Short of a genetic test, there is no way to know if Fersen or King Louis XVI fathered the children, but whatever their parentage, both Sophie and Louis Charles died young.

When the eldest son of the King and Queen of France died, the title of Dauphin transferred to the younger Louis Charles. The latter and his sister Marie Therese were the only royal children to survive to the French Revolution with their parents, but the princess would be the only royal heir to reach adulthood.

In 1789, just months after the death of baby Sophie, the royal family was confronted at Versailles by a mob who demanded they vacate Versailles for the Tuileries Palace in Paris. There, the royals were kept under lock and key, watched daily by guards and regularly searched for letters moving in and out of the palace. Marie Therese and Louis Charles spent the majority of their time with their mother, under watchful eyes. In September of 1791, France's revolutionists declared the monarchy illegal and the country a republic; the next year, the Bourbon's were taken forcefully from their home and imprisoned in the Temple.

An already centuries-old fortress, the Temple was used as a prison in the 18th and 19th centuries for notable members of the nobility. It no longer exists, but **from 1792 to 1793 it was home to Louis Charles** and his family, until the boy was given into the care of Antoine Simon and Marie-Jeanne. Coerced into confession at his mother's trial, Louis Charles told the court that he had been abused at the hands of his family members—testimony that was used to condemn the queen. Afterward, the ten-year-old boy became sick and eventually died in captivity.

The remaining royalists in France refused to believe that Louis Charles, considered King after the death of his father, was truly dead; rumors circulated that the boy had escaped. Modern **DNA testing of the heart** of the presented corpse—preserved in 1795—concludes that the body was indeed that of Louis Charles.

As for Marie Therese, she survived her imprisonment in the Temple and was freed in the last month of 1795. She traveled directly to Austria, the birthplace of her mother and home of the Holy Roman Emperor Francis II, her cousin. In exile, she agreed to marry her cousin Louis Antoine, son of her father's eldest surviving brother, in 1799. When Napoleon I abdicated in 1814, Marie Therese's uncle became King Louis XVIII of France under the Bourbon restoration.

Chapter 10 – The Diamond Necklace Scandal

Before his death, Louis XV had commissioned an extravagant diamond necklace for his mistress, Madame du Barry. He wanted the necklace to outshine everything else at court, so Louis spent 2 million French livres to have it created by jewelers Boehmer and Bassenge. The infamous necklace, when completed, contained **647 diamonds and weighed 2,800 carats**. There were multiple ribbons, embellished tassels, bows, and finely cut diamond faces that would have made aristocrats in any nation but France blush.

The problem was, it had taken so long for the jewelers to source so many high-quality diamonds and construct the giant piece of jewelry that when they were finished, the king was dead and his mistress had been banned from the Palace of Versailles in disgrace.

This left Boehmer and Bassenge with an unprecedentedly extravagant necklace, no payment, and no buyer. Their best hope lay with the new Queen of France, Marie Antoinette. Louis XVI offered his wife the necklace but she declined the proposed gift— perhaps because it had been designed for du Barry, a woman she had never liked. So, she replied, **the money would be better spent on equipping a man-of-war** (a battleship.)

Not only were the nearly-bankrupt jewelers becoming desperate to sell their masterpiece, but the mere existence of that sparkling, endearing fortune in the form of a necklace was too much for court manipulators to resist. A distant relation to the French crown, Jeanne de la Motte, thought she could take advantage of a number of factors surrounding the necklace to come away with enough money to make it worth her while. She began by lying to her lover, the Cardinal de Rohan.

The Cardinal had formerly been a French ambassador to the court of Vienna, Austria, and he'd reported regularly on the affairs of Marie Antoinette to her Austrian mother. The French queen was not impressed by this, nor was she happy about one particular report in which the cardinal had mentioned Princess Marie Therese. Whatever the subject of that report, de Rohan felt he had a long way to go to make up with his queen and he genuinely desired to do so. When his mistress, de la Motte, told him she was an intimate friend of the queen, he believed he could use her to endear him to Marie Antoinette.

De la Motte, for her part, pretended to foster an intricate relationship between the cardinal and the queen by appearing to pass letters back and forth between the two parties. Marie Antoinette never actually received the cardinal's letters, let alone replied to them. The forgeries were written by Rétaux de Villette, a notorious blackmailer and prostitute who erroneously signed the letters "Marie Antoinette de France." Evidently, no one involved in the scheme—including Cardinal de Rohan—realized that French royals only sign their first names.

The purpose of the scheme was to get Cardinal de Rohan to believe that Queen Marie Antoinette trusted and liked him so that the former would entrust funds to their apparent go-between without hesitation. The conspirers crafted letters in which the queen seemed to ask for money from the cardinal, in support of her many charities. He handed it over happily, glad to be on her good side. In fact, he believed their friendship was progressing so well that the queen might actually be in love with him. He asked Jeanne de la Motte to arrange a meeting in person with her majesty, so she hired a prostitute that resembled the queen and had the two meet up at night in the gardens. The cardinal was completely fooled.

Seeing that her victim was ripe for the plot, de la Motte gave him a letter in which she made it seem the queen wanted to buy the famous necklace, but without the public knowing. De Rohan was asked to purchase it on behalf of the queen and deliver it to her go-between: Jeanne de la Motte. He did so happily, using the letters as proof of the queen's intention. He arranged to pay by installments with the jewelers and departed with the 2-million livre necklace. Afterward, the cardinal met with a man he expected was a royal representative; the latter rushed the necklace away never to be seen again.

When the jewelers approached Marie Antoinette for payment, the plot was uncovered—but not before the public assumed the worst. It seemed that the queen, already considered a greedy spendthrift woman, had either attempted to buy the lavish necklace in secret or that she had arranged for it to be stolen for her. Neither conclusion was favorable.

In her memoirs, **Madame Campan** explained that despite the culpability of Jeanne de la Motte and her conspirators—who were tried and literally branded as thieves—it was the reputation of Marie Antoinette that suffered the most from the diamond necklace scandal:

> The cardinal was acquitted. Madame de Lamotte (sic), condemned, exposed, and saved only by flight, hastened to publish a pamphlet of the most odious description against the Queen. From that period, so fatal to Marie Antoinette, until her death attacks of this species were incessantly renewed against her. Party spirit lent force to them; the press and the arts lent themselves with equal subservience to the fury of her enemies. Obscene prints, licentious verses,

infamous libels, atrocious accusations I have seen all, I have read all, and I wish I could add (like that unfortunate Princess, on one of the most honorable occasions of her life) I have forgotten all.

Chapter 11 – Queen of Fashion

The most enduring part of Marie Antoinette's legacy is her sense of style. Though her fashions are centuries old, the luxurious collection of fabrics, ruffles, bows, ribbons, and tassels still captures the imaginations of modern designers. The French queen couldn't have known that her wardrobe would leave such a lasting impression on the world, especially given her status as a despised queen. Nevertheless, the Palace of Versailles continues to curate fashion exhibits for men and women in memory of the irreplaceable, highly-stylized Marie Antoinette.

In contemporary times, of course, the queen often struggled to explain what she believed was the necessity of her huge fashion expenditures—especially to her own mother.

As a **letter from Marie Theresa of Austria** notes:

> As you know, I have always been of the opinion that fashions should be followed in moderation but should never be taken to extremes. A beautiful young woman, a graceful queen, has no need for such madness. On the contrary, simplicity of dress is more befitting and more worthy of a queen. I love my little queen and watch everything you do and feel I must not hesitate to draw your attention to this little frivolity.

Despite her mother's discouraging words, Marie Antoinette continued not only to follow French fashions but to further shape the direction in which women's styles were developing. One of the most important changes the young French Dauphine made to the nation's fashion was to wear patterned fabrics instead of the plain ones promoted by King Louis XV.

It wasn't exactly rebellious on her part; the French courtesans who accompanied the former Austrian princess across the border dressed her in a patterned gown right from the start. Nevertheless, she embraced fully-printed fabrics with her whole heart, as did the French aristocracy, which did nothing to dissuade the French public from buying Indian prints or knock-offs. This popularity made the eventual end of the Fabric Wars inevitable.

Though it may be difficult for the modern eye to discern much difference between the average late-18th-century aristocratic dress and one belonging to Marie Antoinette or her followers, the differences were quite stark to the Queen's contemporaries. Many of the queen's fashions were designs from Rose Bertin, a woman who favored low, breast-hugging necklines and flowing gown hems that revealed the ankles.

Bertin is one of the first designers in France to have received international acclaim, and she owed her success to the patronage of Marie Antoinette and her ladies-in-waiting. Though the milliner-by-trade was reasonably successful before the new queen took the throne, once Marie Antoinette became queen Bertin visited the Palace of Versailles twice a week to show off new dresses to the ladies and take orders.

Rose Bertin is most famous for her Polish-style dresses, known at Marie Antoinette's court as *robes a la Polonaise*. It wasn't the first time France—or Versailles—had seen Polish style. Louis-Auguste's mother, Queen Maria Leczinska, was from Poland and she had worn fashions from her native country decades before her son's wife.

Les robes a la Polonaise not only featured low necklines and shorter hems but an entire extra section at the back of the skirt that could be left low or draped and gathered like a bustle. In the last quarter of the 18th century, this particular dress was found on every member of Marie Antoinette's retinue at some point during the week. She also had a love of English-style dresses, which shared similar construction to the Polish dress style.

The Queen of France bonded with Rose Bertin to the extent that the designer not only created countless beautiful dresses for her but also collaborated with her hair stylist to create an entire, cohesive look. Leonard-Alexis Autie was the favorite hairdresser of the queen, but not immediately. When Marie Antoinette moved to Versailles, Autie was working with Madame du Barry—two years later, he was in the Dauphine's apartments styling her hair.

Autie and Bertin were the power team behind Marie Antoinette, in terms of style. As the Dauphine, and later the queen, Marie knew that the court looked to her to uphold the high fashion standards of Versailles and all France—but she also came into that position as a teenage foreigner who worried about how she would be received. She was a strong and social person who at first did as she was told; the more time that passed and the more she learned about the culture in which she found herself, the more Marie imposed her own will on the society around her. She wanted to be seen as a real force of power within Versailles, though she had no real authority as a woman.

The Dauphine, upon first entering Versailles, found to her immense distaste that every morning and night she was to be dressed and undressed by a team of noble ladies. She accepted this for a time, but when her full confidence had returned, she threw the ladies out and left her clothing and hair in the hands of Bertin and Autie. It was a bold move not only because the former method was traditional but because her chosen stylists were not of noble blood. Nevertheless, Marie Antoinette became the Queen of France and therefore her stylists stayed with her.

Literally speaking, Autie was the one who worked with the queen's hair, adding wigs and pieces to create the volume that she was, and still is, known for. The architecture of Marie Antoinette's hair, however, was a joint project between the queen herself, Autie, and Bertin. They collectively decided that the royal woman's hair should break free of the classic style that pervaded Versailles at that time, which was heavily powdered and ringleted. Though Marie Antoinette was not averse to curls, and certainly not to powder, she enjoyed experimenting with her hair and using it as a sort of medium in which to express her personality.

Perhaps the most famous of Marie Antoinette's hairstyles is the immense pouf, **up to three or four feet in height** thanks to wigs, fixative, and a lot of hairpins. She also liked to affix decorations in her tall hairdos, from jewels and feather to a fleet of ships. Beyond her own ladies-in-waiting, Marie Antoinette's style choices influenced all youthful ladies of the court who felt compelled to support the Dauphine/Queen and show their appreciation of her. Though the old guard would have nothing to do with such an excess of accessories, ruffles, feathers and clashing colors, teens and young ladies were fascinated with them.

Today, fashion designers, stylists, and consumers are still mesmerized by the decadence of those 18th-century gowns, shoes, and presentations. **Modern fashion collections** found on the runways of New York, Milan, and of course Paris, often embody the spirit and aesthetic of late 18th-century Versailles. As for off-the-rack clothing options, the French queen's Bohemian style has persisted almost without pause since Marie Antoinette herself strolled the gardens of Petit Trianon wearing soft, simple peasant clothing.

The idealistic characterization of Marie Antoinette in an ornate, ruffled gown printed with flowers or stripes and adorned with silk ribbons is, for many, the pinnacle of both women's fashion and luxurious indulgence. The queen's wardrobe was akin to a box of fine, ornate chocolates or a hot scented bath topped with rose petals.

The last French queen remains a style icon whose bold choices have still impacted the way women dress—more than 200 years after her death.

Chapter 12 – The French Revolution

The French population was poor and hungry when Louis XVI became king, and it was still the same ten years after he'd taken his father's place on the throne. All the charity organizations, the free evening meals, and the insistence from Louis-Auguste that he wanted to do as the public desired weren't enough to keep the rising population happy. By the end of the 1780s, peasants and small landowners were demanding more.

Along with more hungry mouths and a slight economic decline in the 1770s, the 18th century had been a time of philosophical enlightenment in France and Europe. There were more educated non-elites in the country than ever before, and these people were asking questions that went against France's tradition of putting the nobility first.

One of the most controversial decisions taken by King Louis XVI—at the insistence of his advisors—was to send military aid to America during its Revolutionary War against Great Britain. The reason for doing so was twofold: Great Britain was France's ancient enemy, and in helping the new United States of America, France was securing a new alliance with a country full of resources. Simultaneously, however, Louis XVI was helping a defiant population rebel against its crown—as such the war effort set a dangerous precedent for France's own monarchy. Additionally, the enormous cost of sending troops, weapons, supplies, and ships to America was more than the already struggling French coffers could take.

Madam Campan describes the atmosphere in France leading up to the Revolution in her memoirs:

> Twenty years before the [R]evolution I often heard it remarked that the imposing character of the power of Louis XIV was no longer to be found in the Palace of Versailles; that the institutions of the ancient monarchy were rapidly sinking; and that the people, crushed beneath the weight of taxes, were miserable, though silent; but that they began to give ear to the bold speeches of the philosophers, who loudly proclaimed their sufferings, and their rights; and, in short, that the age would not pass away without the occurrence of some grand shock, which would unsettle France, and change
>
> the course of its progress.

Louis-Auguste and Marie Antoinette were not despotic rulers who believed their subjects should work hard, eat little, and pay higher and higher taxes their entire lives; in 1789, the king decided to summon the Third Estate itself (common people) and try to come up with some solutions for the peasantry. He also planned a meeting with the First and Second Estates (clergy and nobility), but he planned each separately, a fact the commoners took personally. They wanted to meet together with the nobles and clergy so as to be taken seriously on equal grounds.

In the 18th century, the French common people had no political power whatsoever. They could not vote for their leaders or provide advice to any governing body. The nobility and the church, however, were ubiquitous forces in the politics of the day, for no more reason than that's how things had been for centuries throughout Europe. The clergy believed they had a right to counsel the throne and remain untaxed because the Catholic church was considered the authority on earthly and spiritual matters. The nobility believed the same because they were taught they had inherited superior bloodlines from their noble ancestors.

Two things happened when the king arranged these three meetings. First, the clergy and the nobility were disgusted at Louis' suggestion that the crown needed to tax the rich and privileged to cover expenses. Second, the Third Estate decided to assemble on their own terms, forming the **National Assembly**. Concerned, the king ordered the Salle des Etats closed on the day the National Assembly planned to convene, weakly claiming that the building was undergoing construction and maintenance. Undeterred, the middle class met on the 17th of June 1789 in a tennis court outside Versailles. They signed the Tennis Court Oath and vowed not to disperse until they had written a formal constitution for the country. In a few days, the National Assembly had the support of most of the clergy as well as 47 members of the nobility.

The monarchs sent in the military but allowed the assembly to persist in meeting at the Salle des Etats. Though no orders were given to make arrests or clear out the meeting space, French and international soldiers continued to pour into Paris and Versailles. Weeks went by, and worried that their demands would not be met, the commoners began to riot in the city. On July 14, after several days of violence, rioters focused their efforts on the most powerful symbol of the monarchy: the Bastille.

The Bastille was an ancient fortress, used contemporarily for the storage of arms and ammunition, as well as for holding high-class prisoners. After a battle of several hours, Governor Marquis Bernard-Rene de Launay ordered a cease-fire; still, the mob rushed the gates, killing him and touting his head on a spike throughout Paris. The National Assembly took advantage of the confusion and chaos to install their own president, **Jean-Sylvain Bailly, Mayor of Paris.**

Meanwhile, Marie Antoinette, Louis-August, and their two children remained at Versailles, purposefully letting the riots run their course before showing their faces or making demands. Their young son and heir to the throne, Louis Joseph, had died only weeks earlier, making Louis Charles the new heir. Unsure of himself, King Louis XVI recalled his troops and went into Paris on June 17. He was met with cheers of "Long live the King" alongside "Long live the Nation." He went to a meeting with the Parisian government that had been organized by the National Assembly and was cordially presented with the *tricolor cockade,* the symbol of the Revolution. He accepted it and returned to his family at Versailles.

The royal family cowered in their palace as courtiers fled Versailles for other European countries. They were in mourning for their son as well as their *ancien regime,* which was being dissembled piece by piece by the Parisian government. Marie Antoinette remained focused on her daughter and son, Marie Therese and Louis Charles. She kept them close while most of the 3000 inhabitants of Versailles—courtiers, royal officials, servants, diplomats—packed their belongings and abandoned the royal family.

Chapter 13 – The October Chapter

Marie Antoinette and her family remained at the Palace of Versailles with servants for several months following the attack on the Bastille in Paris. They spent their time listening to reports of the new parliament and the goings-on of the National Assembly. For a time, Louis XVI probably expected that his reign and absolute rule would be restored in good time—unfortunately for his family, that was not what the assembled commoners wanted for their future as a nation.

Though a formal French constitution had not yet been agreed upon, on 27 August the Declaration of the Rights of Man was adopted. While this document was being debated and French land divided among the poor, the royal family languished until October 5, 1789.

This time, it was a mob of common women who marched towards a bastion of France's ancien regime, furious about the lack of bread and the high prices of those loaves that were available. Their shouts and riotous anger mixed with the revolutionary spirit of politicians and commoners in their midst. Many more joined the women over the hours it took them to walk from Paris to Versailles, until there were tens of thousands of protestors at the gates of the palace. In an effort to solve the problem, guards allowed six women into the palace to speak directly with the king.

A witness to the fray, **Stanislas Maillard**, described the scene for posterity:

> ...in the middle of the Champs Elysées...he saw
> detachments of women coming up from every
> direction, armed with broomsticks, lances, pitchforks,
> swords, pistols, and muskets. As they had no
> ammunition, they wanted to compel him to go with a
> detachment of them to the arsenal to fetch powder,
> but. . . now by means of prayers and protestations he
> succeeded in persuading the women to lay down their
> arms, with the exception of a few who refused, but
> whom wiser heads among them compelled to yield.

The six women marched into the palace and confronted Louis XVI, whom they afterward claimed was quite charming and affable. The king gave the women permission to distribute bread from the royal stock and promised there would be more to come. The mob dispersed, mollified for the time being. When no more bread appeared, the women knew who to blame: Marie Antoinette. They expected she had changed her husband's mind about providing bread for his people—and they were not prepared to let her get away with such treachery.

The crowd continued to swell as the day progressed, so in a last-ditch effort to pacify his people, King Louis XVI announced that he accepted the Declaration of the Rights of Man. It was not enough to calm the growing crowds. Furthermore, there were too few guards posted at the palace to deal with the swarm of people, a fact that undoubtedly contributed to the eventual comradery between the protesting women and palace guards. The latter knew they stood no chance against the crowd and therefore generally opted to be friendly and understanding towards the protestors. It was the right move to make.

As the hours wore on, Marie Antoinette, Louis-Auguste and their children remained in the palace while the sunset and people outside continued to shout and look for a way inside. Around six o'clock in the morning, October 6, members of the crowd noticed a small, unguarded gate that led to the palace. Swiftly they entered the home of the French royal family and began searching for Marie Antoinette's bedchamber to ransack it. As soon as the breach was discovered, royal guards panicked. They swept the halls and shut every door within the palace, locking every internal entranceway in an effort to keep the trespassers at bay. When guards saw people in the hall, they opened fire; **a young intruder was killed**.

When the crowd outside understood what had happened, there was no turning back. Hundreds and then thousands pushed their way inside the palace, killing and decapitating two of the guards along the way.

The queen heard the commotion and ran with her ladies to the king's bedchamber. Louis-Auguste had the door locked and wasn't sure whether it was his wife or the rioters at the door; the queen and her retinue were admitted just ahead of the angry crowd. They cowered in the bedroom until a Parisian soldier, the Marquis de Lafayette, intervened with the royal guards, his own Paris troops, and the crowd. With the people calmed considerably, Lafayette led the king out onto an inner balcony within view of the crowd. Louis-Auguste gave in to their demands and promised to accompany them to Paris.

The king's statement wasn't enough to please the rioters. They demanded to see the queen, whom Lafayette produced alongside the Dauphin and princess Marie Therese. She was quiet and respectful, standing with her arms crossed over her chest as many armed rioters leveled muskets towards her. They called for the children to be removed, ostensibly to keep them safe from the oncoming attack upon the queen, but after a moment the weapons were lowered. Marie Antoinette remained in place, frightened for her life and at the mercy of the tens of thousands of rioters around her. Seeing his opportunity to save her, Lafayette responded to the heavily sympathetic atmosphere and bent down to kiss the queen's hand. She was safe, as was her family—but she was no longer free. From that moment on, the Bourbons of France were hostages of the middle class.

Several hours later, Marie Antoinette, Louis-August, and the royal children climbed into a carriage and rode slowly into Paris. They were escorted by 100 loyal servants and deputies from Versailles and marched along by a crowd that had swelled to 60,000 in size. The journey from their home to Paris took a long nine hours, at the end of which Louis and his family were installed in the Tuileries Palace. It had been left virtually untouched since the reign of King Louis XV.

Chapter 14 – Anxious Days at the Tuileries

It pleased the French greatly to have their monarch in the capital city, where they believed he would be face-to-face with the trials and difficulties of the common folk and be better able to fix them. The newly-created offices of Mayor of Paris and others remained, however, and so in this way Louis XVI was expected merely to do his duty as the head administrator of the country. He was no longer allowed to leave Paris. Marie Antoinette, for her part, could do nothing but stay inside the broken-down castle and keep a close eye on her children.

The first thing Louis-Auguste did upon their forced stay at the Tuileries was to declare, "It is always with pleasure and with confidence that I find myself amidst the inhabitants of my good city of Paris." He then installed himself at the Tuileries and immediately asked a servant to **bring him a book on England's Charles I**—a monarch who had been forced from the throne of England, Scotland, and Ireland and ultimately executed more than a century earlier. He knew that his was not a good position.

The atmosphere at the Tuileries was very strange, in that though the Royals were essentially captives, they were also still given royal privileges such as furniture and clothing couriered from Versailles.

The household remained intact with enough loyal servants to clean the old castle and organize sleeping quarters for everyone. Part of the gardens were separated and made private for the family; Marie Antoinette frequented these with her son and daughter.

Though the Royals were comfortably-accommodated, they were not naïve enough to believe themselves out of danger. Their correspondence was monitored, however, and it was not easy to send a message outside of the Tuileries to someone who might be able to help the family. Marie Antoinette and Louis-Auguste bided their time, maintaining an air of calm authority over the throngs of people who clamored around the Tuileries for a glimpse of the royal faces. From under the windows of the royal apartments, **voices reached up**

to Marie Antoinette at all hours.

> *'Send away from you,' said one, 'all these courtiers who ruin kings. Love the inhabitants of your good city.'*
>
> *'I loved them at Versailles,' replied the Queen, 'I will love them just the same at Paris.'*
>
> *'Yes, yes,' said another; "but on the fourteenth of July you wanted to besiege the city and have it bombarded.'*
>
> *'You were told so,' answered the Queen, 'and you believed it. It was that which caused the woes of the people and of the best of kings.'*
>
> *A third woman addressed the sovereign in German.*
>
> *'German!' said Marie Antoinette; 'I no longer understand it. I have become so thorough a French-woman that I have even forgotten my mother tongue.'*
>
> *There was a burst of applause. The women asked the Queen for the flowers and ribbons on her bonnet. She*

unfastened them herself and gave them away. The throng cried, 'Long live our good Queen!'

The crowds were much more affectionate towards the Queen of France when they could see her in person; of course, it helped that the food crisis had been abated and the city's bakeries were no longer packed with long lines of customers who demanded more bread than was available. Marie Antoinette's best friend, the Princess de Lamballe, re-entered the city when she heard what had happened at Versailles and was sure to host regular parties so that the queen would have good reason to leave the palace. After one appearance, however, the queen felt it was better to remain at her own estate to avoid being further judged as frivolous.

The family lived at the Tuileries from October 1789 to August of 1792, and the royal parents did what they could to shield their young children—just eleven and four years old when forcibly evicted from Versailles—from the fear and insecurity they felt. Although, comparatively, the king was considerably less anxious than his wife. Once they were installed at their new home, he continued to meet with city leaders, diplomats, and department heads as if the entire fabric of France had not drastically shifted. It was Marie and their young son who seemed to suffer the most.

The queen was often seen with red, puffy eyes, and the Dauphin had begun to suffer from nightmares since the endless night at the Palace of Versailles. None of the family could let themselves be seen at the windows of the Tuileries without having insults or lewd comments thrown at them from people outside. Tensions without the household were so high that at any moment the family and guards expected the worst.

The king's younger sister, Madame Elisabeth, later recalled that one night someone woke up screaming from a nightmare and the entire shift of palace guards also began to scream in fear. The situation was far from comfortable, but there was very little Marie Antoinette could do to change her circumstances. She spent time with her little boy and girl, walked in the little private section of their garden, and tried to make them feel at home. In addition to her own children, the queen was caring for Ernestine Lambriquet, an orphan of former palace servants. The girl had been legally adopted by Marie Antoinette and Louis-Auguste, and she shared a room with Marie Therese.

The other adopted children were placed in convents and boarding schools at the onset of the Revolution, with the exception of a boy called **Armand**. Nearly twenty, the former peasant boy is said to have left the royal family at the onset of the Revolution. Ernestine remained with her adopted family throughout the trials at Versailles and the Tuileries, side-by-side with Marie Therese.

With three children in her physical care and many more depending on her school and boarding payments elsewhere, Marie Antoinette was desperate to find a way to get her family out of harm's way. Help presented itself in a curious way.

Chapter 15 – An Attempt to Flee

Count Hans Axel von Fersen believed it was absolutely necessary for the royal family to leave the Tuileries before more harm could be done to them. He planned an escape for them with the Baron von Breteuil after receiving confirmation that Swedish King Gustavus III offered his support to the French monarchs. Von Fersen wanted the king, queen, princesses, and the Dauphin to dress in costume to exit the Tuileries and then climb into two waiting carriages to travel quickly to Montmedy, a fortress near the France-German border (now the France-Belgium border.)

Von Fersen convinced Marie Antoinette that the escape attempt was their best chance at survival, but she had a difficult time persuading Louis-Auguste to undertake the journey. The king still believed that if he performed his duties to the people, he and his family would be safe and, in time, revered once more. The queen insisted, however, and her husband respected her wishes. They planned to make their exit on June 21, 1791, one and a half years after the family had been forced out of Versailles.

The first step was to disguise the royal family well enough that the guards at the palace wouldn't notice. It was decided to dress all three children—Louis Charles, Marie Therese and Ernestine—as girls, which was easy enough as the Dauphin was not yet six years old. The queen herself would act as their governess, wearing a plain black dress. The king would act as valet, donning the coat and hat of a regular visitor to the palace. His sister Elisabeth acted as the mother of the children, putting on a Russian accent to confuse any onlookers.

Von Fersen wanted the family to split up into two light carriages once they had slipped out of the palace in disguise, simply because two lighter vehicles with fewer passengers would be much quicker on the road. Once inside, the family would be driven as quickly as possible to several checkpoints on the way to Montmedy, where von Fersen had arranged pro-monarchy military supporters to meet them.

Marie Antoinette, however, was uncomfortable splitting up the family into two coaches. She refused to separate herself from Louis-Auguste and insisted that everyone travel together. Unable to convince her otherwise, von Fersen gave into Marie Antoinette's demands and produced a large, heavy carriage to carry the king and queen, three children, and himself. The coach required six horses to pull it and was much more conspicuous and slow than the family's co-conspirator would have liked, but he followed through with his plan as best he could.

On the appointed day, the Royals put on their disguises secretly and successfully left the Tuileries behind them. Unfortunately, the queen was late to the coach. Because she had stopped leaving the palace long ago, she was unfamiliar with the surrounding streets and alleyways; Marie Antoinette was lost as soon as she left the estate. She hurried through the streets in a panic, the clock ticking, and finally found the waiting carriage with everyone inside. They departed immediately.

The escape party could have easily made up for lost time if the family had agreed to travel in separate carriages, but as it was, the single coach moved slower than anything else on the road. Steadily, the monarchs and von Fersen pulled away from Paris and left it altogether; their schedule, however, was ruined. Few remained at the checkpoints to greet them, change horses, and move them safely onward; either the people posted had been frightened off by gathering crowds or they assumed the plan was unsuccessful from the beginning.

Probably the worst part of an already poorly-executed escape plan was the attitude of Marie Antoinette and Louis-Auguste, who seemed to lose all sense of urgency once they had left Paris. The king mistakenly believed that the revolutionaries of France were confined to Paris, so he openly confided and trusted in the peasants he met along the road from the capital to Montmedy. Marie Antoinette did the same, happily chatting with helpful people on the road and giving them gifts from luggage she'd packed into the coach.

In nearly every little village along the way, the king and queen were out of the vehicle, soaking in the blessings of the common people. It must have been such a welcome change from the harassment and insults in Paris; perhaps the overwhelmed monarchs just couldn't help but indulge in the warm welcomes that awaited them outside the city.

Unfortunately, all the conversations and unforeseen repairs to the heavy coach took an enormous toll on the schedule. The royal party had traveled as far as Sainte-Menehould, 220 kilometers from the Tuileries, when a pro-revolutionary post-master **matched the apparent valet's face to a piece of paper money** and notified the Parisian guards who by that time were on the road searching for the escaped monarchs. Less than 25 kilometers down the road, at Varennes-en-Argonne, the escape party was captured. It was 11:00 p.m. on 21 June, and they were about 30 kilometers from Montmedy. Germany was just beyond.

At the insistence of the army, the royal party turned around the next morning and returned to Paris. Fortunately, Count Axel von Fersen was not implicated in the escape attempt because the king had asked him to quit the coach earlier on the journey; Louis-Auguste wanted to take full responsibility for the journey.

Back in Paris, people were furious that the royals had attempted to leave the burgeoning republic, when for so long the king had seemed to make every effort to work with the people's government. And yet, at the Tuileries, not a word was said about the affair. **Jerome Petion**, part of the armed escort back to Paris, was confused by the decorum of the king and his servants after what must have been a horrifying experience:

> After a few minutes, we moved [to] the king's apartments. Already all valets were in attendance, wearing their usual court dress. It seemed as if the king had merely returned from a hunting expedition, and everyone was assisting him with his toilet. In seeing the king, in observing him closely, it was impossible to guess that something momentous had just happened. He was so phlegmatic and tranquil, as if nothing was out of the ordinary. He immediately resumed his state of representation. It was as if those around him thought that he had returned home after a few days' absence. I was perplexed by what I saw.

There would be no further attempts to escape, nor any reprieve given the royal family on the part of the Tuileries guards.

Chapter 16 – Death of the Monarchy

When the royals were installed at the Tuileries once more, their privileges—pretended or otherwise—were gone. There was no more privacy, no more pretense of unopened mail, no more leaving the grounds. As before, King Louis XVI got on with the business of state. His wife and children, however, were more anxious and frightened than before. Twice over the next year, threatening mobs broke into the palace but were ultimately calmed by the authoritative presence and speech of the king.

The most shocking development was witnessed in Marie Antoinette herself. Following her humiliating and life-threatening capture outside the German border, the queen's hair is said to have turned completely white. The phenomenon is still known as Marie Antoinette syndrome; the same thing apparently happened to England's Thomas More before he was executed in 1535.

King Louis had no choice but to approve the country's new constitution on 3 September 1791, as it was his only chance to keep the monarchy relevant as France moved into the future. It didn't do him much good, unfortunately, since just over a year later, on September 21, 1792, the people's assembly decided to completely abolish the monarchy. France was a republic; it was at war with Austria and had been threatened by Prussia. The country was completely in chaos, but one thing the majority agreed on was that it was time to move on as an independent country.

A month before the biggest political decision in France's history, Marie Antoinette and the rest of the royal family were arrested and taken from their home once more. This time, the Bourbons were placed into the Temple, the ancient aristocratic prison of Paris. There was no more coddling and no more comfort except the simple fact that the family was together. The Temple was cold, damp, and full of prying soldiers and spies. They huddled together uncomfortably for five months until the National Convention—borne of the National Assembly—condemned King Louis-Auguste XVI to death for the crime of conspiring against France. It was true; the king had been corresponding with Austria, Germany, Sweden, and other nations in the hopes that a defeat of the Republican military would cause France to rethink its previous ruling against the monarchy. Austria was already fighting, but troops were much too far away to help Louis on January 21, 1793, when he faced the executioner.

It was customary to say a few words before bowing to the great machine, but the crowds were so thick and loud that it was impossible for most to hear anything the departing king said from the platform. The Abbe Edgeworth could hear some of what was said by Louis, and he recorded it in his **memoirs**:

> I die innocent of all the crimes laid to my charge; I
> Pardon those who have occasioned my death; and I
> pray to God that the blood you are going to shed may
> never be visited on France.

The king's executioners wore oversized tricolor ribbons on hats they refused to remove in reverence to the monarch. Louis, for his part, tried to remain poised and respectable. The executioners at the guillotine made it difficult as they roughly prepared him to receive the blade. When the sharp and heavy edge of the guillotine blade finally slid down to end the king's life, it made a crooked job of it. Instead of slicing the head off cleanly through the neck, it cut through the back of the head and jaw. The executioner who stood beside the basket picked the head up by its hair and let the blood drip for a long moment in front of the thousands who crowded towards him.

Marie Antoinette and the children were still inside the Temple, but the queen knew of her husband's fate. She remained in the Temple for nine long months after Louis's death, in the end separated from Marie Therese and Louis Charles. Ernestine had been sent away to safety by the queen before her imprisonment, but Marie Therese was cruelly kept away from her mother, and the young boy was put into the custody of Antoine Simon. Rulers of the new French republic wanted Louis Charles, considered by royalists to be King Louis XVII, to be raised as a fierce republican. His upbringing with the Simons was anything but luxurious, but most accounts show that the young boy was well taken care of.

The government of the commune—France's temporary title following its deposed monarchy—was attempting to make a firm case against the former queen. In obtaining the testimony from the nine-year-old Louis, the commune had what they needed. The queen's child, confused and manipulated endlessly, signed a declaration that said Marie Antoinette had molested and abused him. More delegations came afterward to question him, but he refused to speak any more to political visitors.

Following the child's testimony, Marie Antoinette was brought to trial on January 14, 1793. She was surprised by the appointment and only given one day to prepare her defense with a lawyer. Over the course of two days, the queen was accused of stealing French money and sending it to Austria; she was also accused of planning the deaths of revolutionary soldiers and abusing her son. Regarding the last accusation, Marie Antoinette would not comment. She was visibly upset at the statements made against her and ultimately was found guilty of high treason against France. When she heard the decision of the court, she returned to her cell and wrote to her sister-in-law, **Elisabeth**.

I WRITE TO YOU, MY SISTER, FOR THE LAST TIME. I HAVE BEEN CONDEMNED, NOT TO AN IGNOMINIOUS DEATH – THAT ONLY AWAITS CRIMINALS – BUT TO GO AND REJOIN YOUR BROTHER. INNOCENT AS HE, I HOPE TO SHOW THE SAME FIRMNESS AS HE DID IN HIS LAST MOMENTS. I GRIEVE BITTERLY AT LEAVING MY POOR CHILDREN; YOU KNOW THAT I EXISTED BUT FOR THEM AND YOU – YOU WHO HAVE BY YOUR FRIENDSHIP SACRIFICED ALL TO BE WITH US.

Marie Antoinette's sentencing was carried out the very day she was found guilty. The queen asked for clean white clothing and dressed herself in view of the guards at the prison. It was traditional for French queens, once widowed, to wear white. Her hair was cut short to accommodate the impending guillotine and her hands bound behind her back. According to **Madame Bault**, wife of the prison warden, the executioner who cut the queen's hair pocketed the shorn locks.

Marie Antoinette was conveyed to the Place de la Revolution in an open cart, a rope around her neck with one end held by a guard. She was denied the privacy of a carriage, as Louis-Auguste had ridden in almost a year earlier. She said little on the platform, save to apologize for stepping on the foot of one of the executioners.

She was killed in the same fashion as her husband, nine months earlier, except that this time the blade cleanly found its mark. When the lady's head was shown to the crowd, they **celebrated** and shouted "**Vive le Republique!**"

Marie Antoinette's young son, Louis Charles, died in captivity at the Temple prison in 1795, but Marie Therese survived and upon her release fled to Austria. She tried desperately to find Ernestine but could find no news of her adopted sister until the Bourbon Restoration in 1814. By then, Ernestine had died.

Count Axel von Fersen never stopped conspiring to save the royal family, but his and the efforts of dozens of royalists were in vain. Louis-Auguste's brother retook the French Throne in 1814, becoming King Louis XVIII. The French monarchy was again—and finally—put aside in 1848.

Marie Antoinette remains an infamous yet highly misunderstood historical figure. She and Louis-Auguste are buried at the Basilica of St. Denis in Paris, together with the heart of their son Louis Charles and the bodies of Princess Sophie and Louis Joseph. Marie Therese, who died in 1851, is buried in Slovenia with her husband.

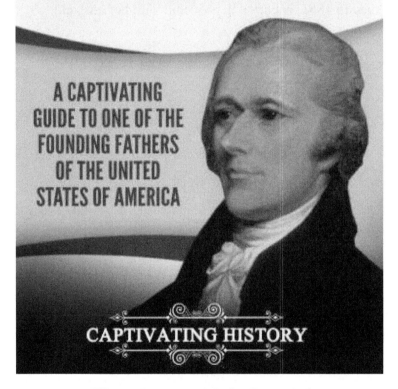

Check out this book!

AARON BURR

A CAPTIVATING GUIDE TO THE LIFE OF AARON BURR AND THE MOST FAMOUS DUEL IN AMERICAN HISTORY

CAPTIVATING HISTORY

Check out this book!

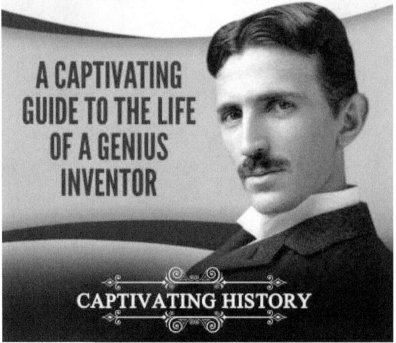

Check out this book!

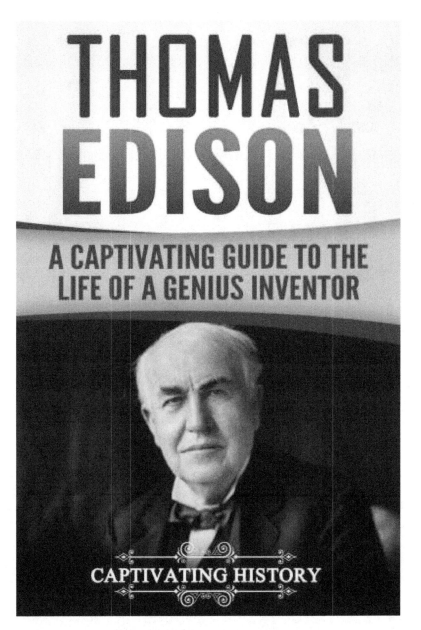

Check out this book!

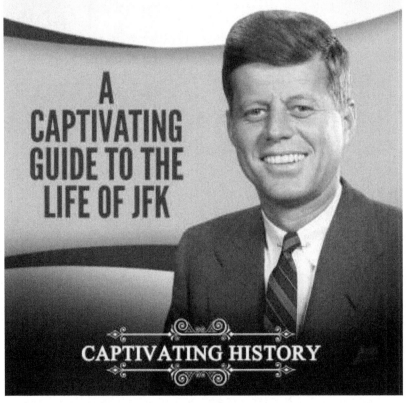

Check out this book!

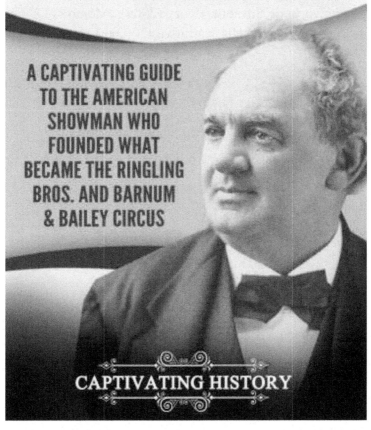

P.T. BARNUM

A CAPTIVATING GUIDE TO THE AMERICAN SHOWMAN WHO FOUNDED WHAT BECAME THE RINGLING BROS. AND BARNUM & BAILEY CIRCUS

CAPTIVATING HISTORY

Check out this book!

Works Cited

Campan, Mme (1909), Memoirs of Madame Campan on Marie Antoinette and her court.

Essex Edgeworth de Firmont, Henry (2009), Memoirs Of The Abbe Edgeworth: Containing His Narrative Of The Last Hours Of Louis XVI (1815).

Farr, Evelyn (2016), I Love You Madly: Marie-Antoinette and Count Fersen: The Secret Letters.

Fraser, Antonia (2002), Marie Antoinette: The Journey.

Lever, Evelyne (2006), Marie Antoinette: The last Queen of France.

Levy, Applewhite and Johnson (eds.) (1979), Women in Revolutionary Paris, 1789–1795.

Saint Amand, Imbert de (1891), Marie Antoinette at the Tuileries, 1789-791.

The Gentleman's Magazine, Volume 46 (1776).

Vons Fersen, Hans Axel (2010), Diary And Correspondence Of Count Axel Fersen V8: Relating To The Court Of France (1902).

Weber, Caroline (2006), Queen of Fashion: What Marie Antoinette Wore to the Revolution.

Weber, Joseph (1805), Memoirs of Maria Antoinetta ... queen of France and Navarre.

Webster, Paul (4 Aug 2002) The Guardian, "Size did matter to Marie-Antoinette.)

Zweig, Stefan (1984), Marie Antoinette: The Portrait of an Average Woman.

Free Bonus from Captivating History (Available for a Limited time)

Hi History Lovers!

Now you have a chance to join our exclusive history list so you can get your first history ebook for free as well as discounts and a potential to get more history books for free! Simply visit the link below to join.

Captivatinghistory.com/ebook

Also, make sure to follow us on:

Twitter: @Captivhistory

Facebook: Captivating History:@captivatinghistory